IMAGES
of America
JEWELL RIDGE
PORTRAIT OF
A COAL TOWN

The "Welcome to Jewell Ridge" sign is more than a direction to the town. It embodies the warm welcome Jewell Ridgers give to visitors. They are proud of their town and its place in history, both when the mining operation was at its peak and now when times are quieter. A sense of belonging to an era when friendship and loyalty and an important work ethic were important seems to be woven into the rich fabric of Jewell Ridge. (Courtesy of Margaret Matney.)

ON THE COVER: Members of the United Mine Workers of America (UMWA) No. 7068 helped with the formation of the Clinch Valley Clinic in Richlands. The clinic and the Jewell Ridge Hospital worked together to serve all the local medical needs. Dr. J. A. Robinson is at center left. Most of the group is unidentified but included (not in order) are believed to be Perry White, Kedric Osborne, Clyde Glover, and Tom Whited. (Courtesy of Ginger Mustard.)

IMAGES
of America

JEWELL RIDGE
PORTRAIT OF
A COAL TOWN

Louise B. Leslie and
Dr. Terry W. Mullins

ARCADIA
PUBLISHING

Published by Arcadia Publishing
Charleston, South Carolina

Library of Congress Catalog Card Number: 2008925019

For all general information contact Arcadia Publishing at:
Telephone 843-853-2070
Fax 843-853-0044
E-mail sales@arcadiapublishing.com
For customer service and orders:
Toll-Free 1-888-313-2665

Visit us on the Internet at www.arcadiapublishing.com

These community matriarchs wait for a local program to begin at the first homecoming celebration on July 4, 1988. They are (from left to right) Madge Jennelle, Cary Altizer, Helen Phipps, Elsie Brown, Audrey Perkins, Narcie Smith, Dorothy Cook, Rachel Whited, and Gladys Smith Newman. In the background are (from left to right) former state senator Jack Reasor, former Tazewell county supervisor Ben Barringer, former delegate Jackie Stump, Dr. Stuart McGehee, Barbara Altizer, Thomas Righter, and Robert Moore. (Courtesy of Rudolph M. Taylor.)

CONTENTS

ACKNOWLEDGMENTS

We sincerely thank all those who helped make this book possible. Hundreds of pictures were contributed to tell the story of Jewell Ridge. Unfortunately all the pictures could not be used due to space limitations or the quality of the photographs submitted. Special appreciation is extended to the Jewell Ridge Recreation and Development Corporation, which initiated the idea for this publication, and to Harry David Taylor, who was a leader in the project and a constant help.

    Contributors include: Loraine Johnson, Katherine Richardson, Carol Mullins, John McClintock Jr., Bill Patton, William P. Keene, Gaynelle Thompson, Ginger Mustard, Margaret Matney, Harry David Taylor, Rudolph Taylor, the Jewell Ridge Archives, Elizabeth Gilbert, John Gilbert, Delores Cox Blankenship, William G. Jackson, Everett Cromer, Mary Elizabeth Jewell Henderson, Lynda Mayhorn, Grubb Photo, Elizabeth Fox Martin, Ellen Elmes, Don Elmes, Barbara Altizer, and Robert Moore. We apologize if any names were inadvertently excluded.

In November 1964, this happy group poses for a picture of close friends and family in the town. They are (first row, from left to right) Willie O. White, Hattie VanDyke Hooker, Ruth Jewell Patton, Tinnie Reynolds, Sally Sparks White (holding baby), and unidentified. In the back are (from left to right) Virgie White Osborne, Lexie VanDyke, Faye Stanley, and Jeanette Anderson. (Courtesy of Ginger Mustard.)

INTRODUCTION

Jewell Ridge stands high astride the Tennessee and Ohio Valley Divide in the northwestern corner of Tazewell County, Virginia. Truly "Tazewell County's Crown Jewel," this community was one of the premier coal camps of the Appalachian region. Like many other coal communities of the 20th century, the work of the coal miner and the life of the coal miner families were challenging and often difficult. The coal miner's job was dangerous. Survivor's benefits, even when miners were killed on the job, did not exist in many operations. However, at Jewell Ridge, the company did provide assistance to families in emergency situations. Coal miner families lived in company houses and were even paid in company currency, or "scrip," which could be spent in the Jewell Ridge company store, as well as at other area businesses. Nevertheless, against this backdrop, a thriving, vibrant mountain community came to life. The quality of life in the coal community was inescapably connected to the respect and fairness shown by the coal mine owners and operators, George W. St. Clair and later his son, Dr. Huston St. Clair. Because of its position at the top of a long ridge separating Tazewell and Buchanan Counties and thanks to the concern and obvious interest its operators showed residents, Jewell Ridge was positioned high above the mines both geographically and symbolically.

In 1902, George W. St. Clair, a Wytheville attorney, moved to Tazewell to practice law. Not long after that event, Thomas M. Righter, a Pennsylvania anthracite coal mine operator, joined St. Clair, and the two opened a coal mine at Jewell Ridge around 1910. A railroad line was then extended to the property, and shortly thereafter, the Jewell Ridge Coal Corporation was chartered. The two men began construction on a community for their employees and their families. Their choice, the highest ridge in their 18,000-acre tract of land, set Jewell Ridge apart from other coal communities. As a result, the community of Jewell Ridge was completed by the Jewell Ridge Coal Corporation by 1915–1916. At an elevation of 3, 500 feet, the coal town was removed from the noise and dust of the coal-mining operations far below. In 1931, young Harley Patrick, a sixth grade student at Jewell Ridge, wrote this descriptive commentary about his hometown:

"The houses are situated on each side of the road. There are about one hundred five houses on the top of the mountain and three other sections of houses called Blacksburg, Newton [sic] and Redtown . . . The houses are painted white and have red and white shingles on top and all of them have numbers on them. Most of the houses have four rooms, but some have three rooms and there are a few that have six and eight rooms."

Eventually, 105 neat, white, frame homes were constructed on either side of a winding road that ran along the ridge of the mountain. Unlike the typical coal town in which houses were clustered in narrow valleys and along creek beds, Jewell Ridge was built high atop a mountain overlooking its neighboring communities.

The Jewell Ridge community included more than just coal company houses, however. Eventually, the town had a school, churches, a post office, a theater, a hospital, a park and ball field, a large company store, and even a clubhouse and a YMCA with a gym located in the center of town. As was the practice in many coal communities, the Jewell Ridge Coal Corporation supplemented teachers' salaries, provided free housing to the educators (often known as "teacherages"), and paid teachers extra to help with community, church, or special summertime activities. As a result, often the best-qualified and most energetic teachers would choose the coal-community schools in which to teach. Jewell Ridge and the immediate area were home to as many as a dozen schools during the first half of the 20th century. Few expenses were spared in making this community a model coal camp.

During the early and mid-20th century, outsiders were often brought to Tazewell County to view state-of-the-art coal communities. One example often used was to take the visitors to Jewell Ridge to see the best that Tazewell County had to offer in coal community development and facilities. In fact, the Jewell Ridge Coal Corporation had its own electric plant and, by 1927, provided electricity to the entire town. In addition, a modern water filtration plant provided clean drinking water. The quality of life for these Jewell Ridge residents was often a great improvement over the lives of their pre-coal industry mountain ancestors. Higher-quality housing and merchandise were the norm for the company town. The arrival of the United Mine Workers of America and the organization of coal miners during the 1930s resulted in improved working and living conditions.

At the conclusion of World War II, the company began to scale its Jewell Ridge operations back. In fact, Tazewell County coal production peaked in 1943 with 4,552 coal miners employed in the county. At that time, the company sold the company houses to private residents of the town. Tons of coal continued to be shipped out of Jewell Ridge. In actuality, by 1990, Tazewell County's principal coal producer was the Jewell Ridge Mine, operated by the Pittston Coal Group. Despite this fact, the Jewell Ridge and other area coal mines saw mechanization greatly decrease the number of men needed to work the mines. As a result, many people with deep roots in the community have been forced to move away. In addition, better roads and the availability of automobiles allowed other coal miners to live farther away from the mines and commute to work. Nevertheless, many current and former Jewell Ridge residents maintain a strong attachment to their coal town, also their hometown. This pride is evident every summer when hundreds and sometimes even thousands gather for the annual Fourth of July celebration and Jewell Ridge Homecoming Festival.

From the air, Jewell Ridge seems to magically appear from within the forested mountaintops of this ridge in the southern Appalachians of southwestern Virginia. This aerial view captures the charm that provides the backdrop for this model coal town. Melvin Grubb, a well-known aerial photographer in the Virginia–West Virginia region, portrayed the unique ambience of the setting in this recent photograph. (Courtesy of Grubb Photo.)

One

FAMILIES ON THE RIDGE

The young family of Whitten and Ellie Clifton Joyce is dressed for some special occasion on the ridge. The children are (from left to right) Walter, Bill, and Oscar Joyce. There was plenty of entertainment for the children and young families in the well-planned community. There were playgrounds, a gymnasium, a YMCA, a bowling alley, a restaurant, a park, a clubhouse, and a theater, in addition to the churches and schools that were the centers of activity. (Courtesy of Loraine Johnson.)

This is a rare photograph of Thomas M. Righter and George W. St. Clair in their early days of developing the mining operation that became the Jewell Ridge Coal Corporation. Pictured are Righter (far left), St. Clair (center), and a young Huston St. Clair. George W. St. Clair's wife is to his right. On the far right is his niece, Virginia St. Clair. This historic picture was made before 1918, the year of Righter's death. The model coal town was largely the vision of St. Clair, who, about 1900, chose the mountaintop site, at 3,500 feet, for a town where the workers and their families could live in a safe and clean environment. Today Jewell Ridge stands as a memorial to George W. St. Clair and his son, Dr. Huston St. Clair, who succeeded his father as president of the corporation. The elder St. Clair died in 1939. Huston St. Clair died in 1974. (Courtesy of Barbara Altizer and Robert Moore.)

Clarence E. Farmer (left) and his brother Millard K. Farmer helped build the new company store following the 1936 town fire. After their original construction job was finalized, they remained in the town and married into the Ratliff family. They and their families became strong supporters and leaders of the Jewell Ridge community. (Courtesy of Harry David Taylor.)

Dr. T. A. Freeman, one of the beloved ministers of the Jewell Ridge Presbyterian Church, worked with the Boy Scout troop and with the church youth. He is pictured in the middle of the group of unidentified young people at a youth camp held at King College in 1949. His wife, the former Virginia St. Clair, taught at the Jewell Ridge School before her marriage. (Courtesy of Carol Mullins.)

Blanch Webb and ? Littlejohn (from left to right, first row) and their husbands, Earl Littlejohn and Layman Webb (from left to right, second row) are ready for church one warm day, perhaps in spring, when the ridges burst with color. One of the well-remembered Presbyterian preachers was Robert Todd Lapsley Liston, who later became president of King College. (Courtesy of Carol Mullins.)

Standing in front of a new 1940 car are (left) Paul Ellis Cook, wearing a new hat; Barbara Cook (center); and Carol Cook. The Cook family was prominent in the early Jewell Ridge community. Young Paul Ellis was a member of the 1945 Vacation Bible School at the Presbyterian church, according to the *Jewell Journal*, an excellent newspaper published by the coal company in the 1940s. J. Howard Miller was the editor and supervisor of the newspaper. (Courtesy of Carol Mullins.)

From left to right, Claire Burke, Otey Anderson, Uva Kennedy, Ruth Anderson, and two unidentified visited in the yard at the Kennedy home on a 1930 summer afternoon on the ridge. Ruth Anderson is remembered for her years of service in the gift shop at the Clinch Valley Clinic. (Courtesy of Carol Mullins.)

This trio stands on the porch of the home of Paul and Dorothy Cook in 1935. The house burned in the 1950s, but the Cook family has pleasant memories of their happy childhood days when (from left to right) Carol Cook, David Burke, and Barbara Cook played with their dolls. (Courtesy of Carol Mullins.)

Paul (left) and Dorothy Burke Cook pose with their children Paul Ellis (on his mother's lap) and Carol at their Jewell Ridge home about 1938. The Cooks and the Burkes were leaders in the community, well remembered for their contributions to the place known worldwide as a model coal camp, where the spectacular views, lush vegetation, and rich natural resources added to its unique stature. (Courtesy of Carol Mullins.)

The Burke family line in Jewell Ridge started with James Burke (1818–1888), who settled on the dividing ridge between the counties of Tazewell and Buchanan. Seated on the front porch of the M. M. Burke home in 1922, from left to right, are the following: (first row) Willie Brewster, Ira Burke, Earl Burke, Dorothy Burke, Clara Burke, Effie Brewster, and Naomi Brewster; (second row) C. R. Burke, Rebecca Burke, Belle Burke, ? Brown, M. M. Burke, and ? Brown. The M. M. Burke home, one of the oldest in the community, was built in 1920. He was a dairyman and farmer who supplied the camp with fresh milk in the 1930s. (Courtesy of Carol Mullins.)

Samantha Ward Christian (left) and A. M. Christian devoted much of their early lives to promoting Jewell Ridge as a thriving community. He helped build the original houses, and she ran the clubhouse for many years. Both the Christians and the Wards have deep roots in southwest Virginia, and their loyalty to Jewell Ridge and its development have remained a strength among their descendants. (Courtesy of Margaret Matney.)

From left to right, Paul Ellis Cook, Barbara Cook, David Burke, and Carol Cook pose in the yard of the M. M. Burke home on Jewell Ridge. They appear to be on their way to Sunday school at the Presbyterian church. (Courtesy of Carol Mullins.)

The John Rufus Joyce family was among the early Jewell Ridge residents who had wide connections in southwest Virginia. Their son is Whitten Joyce, and their granddaughter is Loraine Joyce Johnson. When the Jewell Ridge mine first opened, the workers came in great numbers from around the world. According to an account by Harry David Taylor, "There were Irishmen, Swedes, Germans, Italians, Scotsmen, Poles, and Americans from the far corners of the continent." (Courtesy of Loraine Johnson.)

Zachary Ward was a pioneer settler at Bearwallow. His great-great granddaughter is Margaret Joyce Matney. The snow falls sooner and deeper each year at Bearwallow, where the residents seem to understand the winter ways of the mountains. The name came from the number of bears that used to "wallow" in its secluded hollows. In 1911, there was a one-room school at Bearwallow with 52 students enrolled. The anonymous teacher wrote: "Luckily, they all never managed to find the school room the same day." (Courtesy of Margaret Matney.)

Stella Christian (left) and Gladys Christian are pictured with Bill Joyce, the son of Whitten Joyce. The Joyce family of Jewell Ridge has many descendants in Tazewell and Buchanan counties. Many of the old families were represented in the 1988 reunion of Jewell Ridgers, when more than 25,000 people attended the four-day event. The Fourth of July fireworks display was part of this great celebration when the mountains and skies sparkled with beauty. (Courtesy of Loraine Johnson.)

Narcie Smith (left) and her sister Bobbie pose for the camera in their early days in Jewell Ridge. The widely connected Smith family has been prominent since the first families settled the ridge. During World War II, Robert M. and Louisa "Aunt Lou" Smith had 10 family members serving in the armed forces at the same time. Sons, grandsons, and sons-in-law included Fred B. Smith, Hobert Smith, Harve Smith, William M. Smith, Leslie Smith, Eugene Smith, Robert H. Smith, Robert Howell, F. Underwood, and Robert Jessee. (Courtesy of Katherine Richardson.)

David Christian and Amanda Elswick Christian (seated) are shown here with the basket of perfect apples. They are surrounded by (from left to right) Laura Ward Altizer, Flora Altizer, Doak Altizer, and Jennie Christian. The Jewell Ridge altitude did much to prevent disease-bearing insects from thriving, and almost-perfect fruits and vegetables were grown on the surrounding farms. This produce was often sold at the store. (Courtesy of Margaret Matney.)

The Jewell Ridge glee club entertained for community and school programs. Members were, from left to right, the following: (first row) Harry Lee Smith, ? Jones, Lola Kennedy, Peggy Taylor, Wayne Rasnake, and Buford Childress; (second row) Juanita Smith Jessee, Margaret Richardons, Gaynelle Wise, Helen Richardson, Helen Draughan, Martha Kennedy, ? Rasnake, and Flora Barnett. (Courtesy of Rudolph M. Taylor.)

Sam Young (left) and Perry White, dressed in their Sunday clothes, are pictured on a postcard when they were young men growing up in Jewell Ridge. Years later, a young student, Christen Stacy, quoted her grandfather, Bill Smith, when he described Sundays in the early camp: "I remember Sunday dinner at mommy and poppy's house. While the women were inside cooking, the men would go outside and talk about coal mining. They would talk about where they had worked that week, the conditions they worked in, and who was loading the most coal." (Courtesy of Ginger Mustard.)

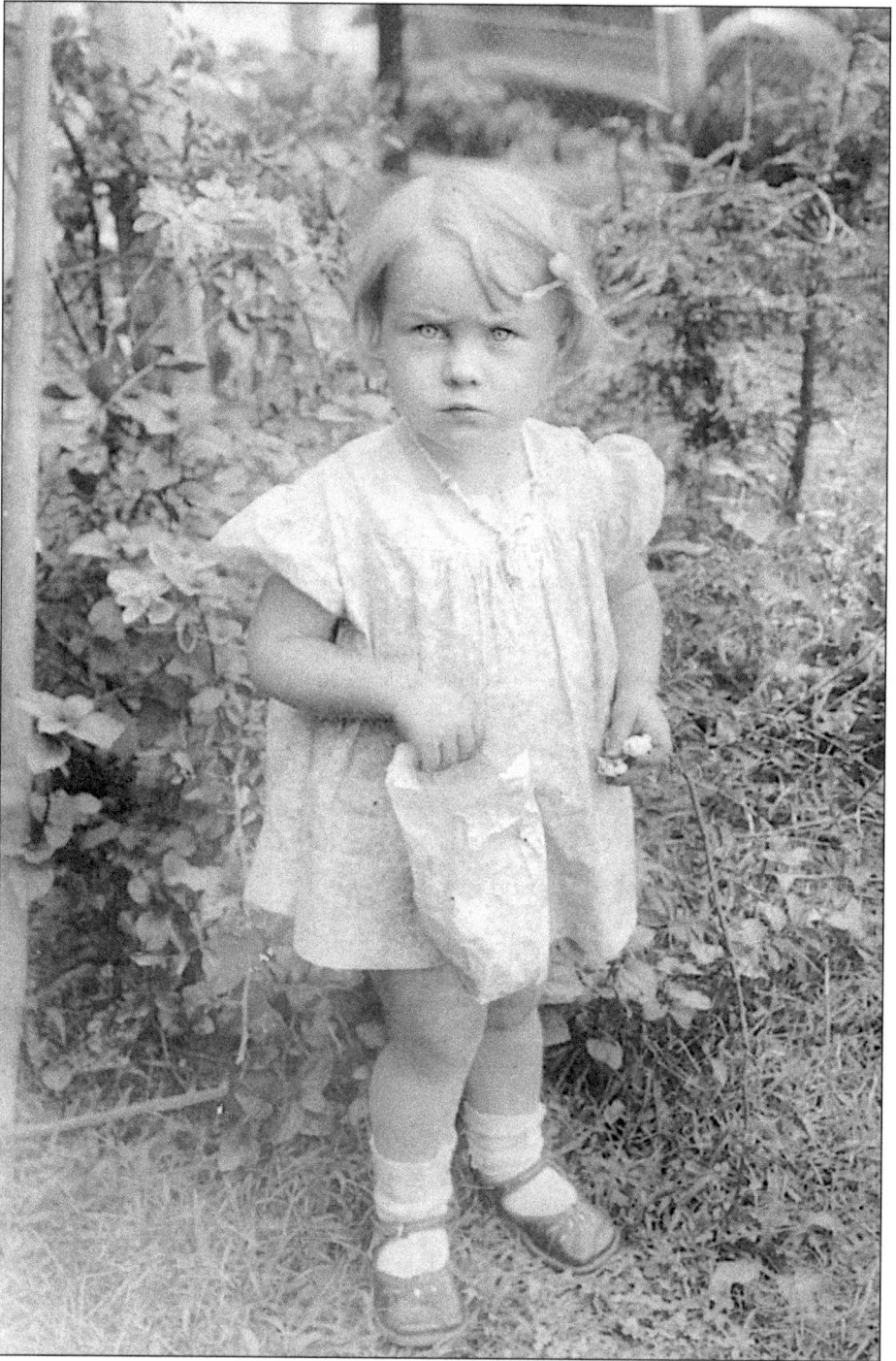

Margaret Joyce (Matney) was one of the children who grew up in the safety of Jewell Ridge, where neighbors took care of each other—in happy and sad times. Pictured here, she had walked to the YMCA to get some popcorn. To ensure safety and cleanliness, George W. St. Clair had cattle guards installed at both ends of the camp to prevent livestock from wandering on the roadways. (Courtesy of Margaret Matney.)

Grandchildren of John Rufus Smith and Susie Ella Smith line up for the photographer in 1933. They are, from left to right, as follows: (first row) Katherine; (second row) Robert, Edith, and Ralph: (third row) Faye and a friend, Rachel Burke. (Courtesy of Katherine Richardson.)

Whitten Joyce (left) and his son Sidney stand together on an important day in the family's life. The family appears to be dressed for a community event, perhaps a wedding. The old mountain custom of treating a newly married couple to a "chivoree," or a serenading, is still remembered, although modern couples seldom follow the tradition. During a chivoree, the groom rides on a fence rail and the bride rides in a washtub. (Courtesy of Margaret Matney.)

Avery Smith was a son of John Rufus Smith and the husband of Narcie Smith. They were well-known leaders on Smith Ridge for many years. This picture was taken in the 1940s. (Courtesy of Katherine Richardson.)

Rader Lewis leaves her home for the walk to school, perhaps on a cool day in autumn. Notice the trees in the front yard. Every early home built in the camp by George W. St. Clair had two Norway maples added to the property. (Courtesy of Jewell Ridge Archives.)

The Gilbert family lived for many years in Jewell Ridge, moved away, and now have returned to their original home. Pictured in 2003 are Robert Gilbert, Ralph "Donnie" Gilbert, Elizabeth Gilbert, and John Gilbert. (Courtesy of Elizabeth Gilbert.)

Susan Beavers (right) has the determined look of many women pictured close to the 1900s, when life in the mountains of southwest Virginia required strength and courage. On the left is her granddaughter Susie Belle Brewster Burke. Susan's ancestry can be traced to the Cherokee Indians who used to live in the local mountain regions (Courtesy of Carol Mullins.)

Elizabeth (left) and Helen Fox, daughters of Lucille and George Fox, seem to be ready for an outing in 1941. Their home on the "Spur" is in the background. The "Spur" was a section of the town away from the center of the community. (Courtesy of Elizabeth Fox Martin.)

Buena Vista Elswick and his large family lived at Stinson Ridge and Jewell Ridge. This picture was taken in 1918 at his Stinson Ridge farm. His unique name came from the town of Buena Vista, Virginia, where his father was fighting during the Civil War when he was notified of the birth of his son. Elswick's wife was Lovicia Reed Elswick, and their children were William, Lottie, Thomas, Powell, Mary Elizabeth, John, James, Wade, Walter, Mayme, Peery, Henry, and Nettie. (Courtesy of Everett Cromer.)

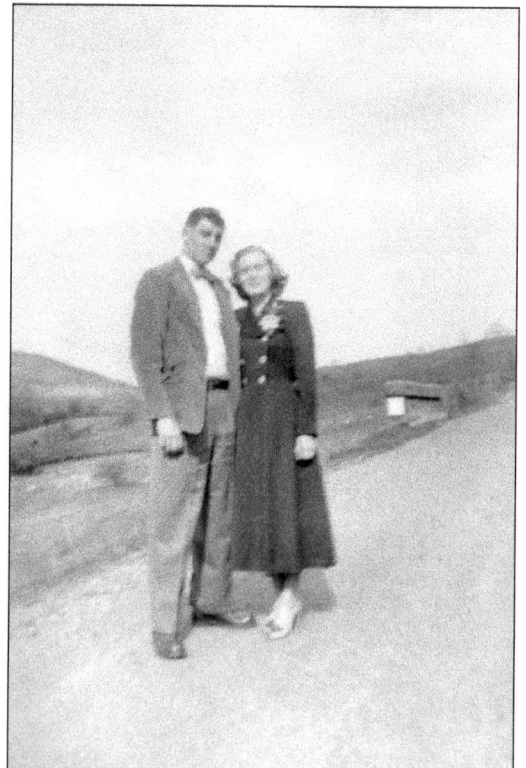

Jim Richardson and Katherine Smith walk along the Jewell Ridge road on a day before their marriage. Jim drove the school bus from Jewell Ridge to Richlands when he was a student at Richlands High School. (Courtesy of Katherine Richardson.)

Ray B. Joyce, a son of Whitten and Ellie Clifton Joyce, served in World War II with the rank of master sergeant. The 1943 editions of the *Jewell Journal*, the biweekly newspaper, are full of news of Jewell Ridge soldiers serving around the globe. One picture in that special section of the *Jewell Journal* is of Sergeant Rider, a son of A. M. and Samantha Christian, who was at Pearl Harbor when the Japanese attacked. (Courtesy of Loraine Johnson.)

Joe Ellis Johnson, the husband of Loraine Joyce Johnson, joined the hundreds who served in the armed forces. In the December 1943 *Jewell Journal*, and in other editions, there is a special section for "our fighting men." Included in that special section of the *Jewell Journal* is a picture of Basom Joyce, son of Whitten Joyce, who was at Pearl Harbor when the Japanese bombs fell. He worked at mine No. 1 at Jewell Ridge before entering the army. (Courtesy of Loraine Johnson.)

Clarence Joyce and his wife, Minnie Chambers Joyce, belong to the large family of Whitten and Ellie Clifton Joyce. The Joyce family was part of the closely knit mine families who lived at Jewell Ridge during the peak of the coal-mining industry. In the late 1920s, the coal corporation employed 650 men and shipped 2,000 tons of coal daily. (Courtesy of Loraine Johnson.)

Whitten Joyce and his wife, Ellie Clifton Joyce, came to Jewell Ridge in the early 1900s. They raised 11 children on the ridge, and their descendants are scattered throughout Tazewell and Buchanan Counties—and beyond. Whitten and Ellie, as well as other early settlers, knew the value of hard work, and they instilled a work ethic in their children. In Jewell Ridge, the hardships of daily living were helped when electricity came to the ridge, at first only at specified times. It is said that by 1927 the electric lights from the camp could be seen from miles away. (Courtesy of Loraine Johnson.)

The family of John L. Keene (1900–1997) and Agnes White Keene lived on Brown Ridge. The large family was pictured in 1948. Included are, from left to right, (first row) Mildred, Agnes, John, and Edna; (second row) Lloyd, Elbert, and Harold; (third row) Frank, Evelyn, Jack, and Bill. Keene worked for the Jewell Ridge Coal Corporation from early youth until 1950, when he accepted a position as a Virginia state mine inspector. (Courtesy of William P. Keene.)

Jim and Katherine Richardson (seated) and their family pose for a modern-day portrait. The children are (from left to right) Julie Edith "Edie," Nancy, Mary Katherine, Bill, Mike, and Sandy. (Courtesy of Katherine Richardson.)

Bill and Gladys Joyce, whose family knew the Jewell Ridge community was unique among coal camps around the globe, probably agreed with Lizzo Brittain, wife of the company doctor, Rufus Brittain, when she said "Jewell Ridge is a community with a soul." Bill and Gladys Joyce had three children: Wilma Jean, Margaret, and Jimmy. (Courtesy of Margaret Matney.)

Narcie Smith (left) and ? Thompson, wife of Clay Thompson, are ready to attend a Jewell Ridge celebration. Clay Thompson was an assistant superintendent of the Jewell Ridge mines. (Courtesy of Katherine Richardson.)

Loraine Joyce Johnson is seen here at the age of 18. She was born in Jewell Ridge, the daughter of Whitten and Ellie Clifton Joyce. The Joyce name is deep in the roots of Jewell Ridge and the surrounding ridges. One teacher at the one-room Smith Ridge School had 37 students, and 10 of them were Joyces. The others had the names of Smith, Addington, and Sparks, and their descendants can still be found on the ridges. (Courtesy of Loraine Johnson.)

Sidney Joyce, the son of Whitten and Ellie Clifton Joyce, is a native of Jewell Ridge. Before the white settlers came to the mountain region in the early 1800s, there were Native American settlements in the area. Three families originally settled Jewell Ridge: the Smiths, Ratliffs, and Burkes. The town of Jewell Ridge, built in the early 1900s, has often been compared to an Alpine village. (Courtesy of Loraine Johnson.)

Bill Joyce lived in the camp at No. 117. All the houses had numbers, and when George W. St. Clair planned the town, he had two Norway maples planted at every home and business. Many of the trees still stand, a monument to his vision of a model coal town. In 1952, Jewell Ridge leaped into the modern era with its excellent television reception at its 3,500-foot elevation. That year, Jewell Ridge had 50 television sets. (Courtesy of Margaret Matney.)

George Fox (left) and Bill Wilson were neighbors on the "Spur" in 1942. They both raised big gardens, and the season's produce is probably the topic of their conversation. (Courtesy of Elizabeth Fox Martin.)

Oscar Robert Joyce, son of Whitten and Ellie Clifton Joyce, was one of the young people who was fortunate enough to attend the excellent schools at Jewell Ridge. Through the years, the Jewell Ridge school system received national recognition for its innovative practices. The kindergarten was of special interest. Preschoolers were invited to choose a can of paint to decorate the individual desks in the colors they liked. The teacher taught from the comfort of a lounge or sofa. Emphasis was on making school a welcoming place. (Courtesy of Loraine Johnson.)

John Luke Jewell and Mary Elizabeth VanDyke were married in 1938. The Jewell and VanDyke families have been part of the Jewell Ridge community since its beginning. The town was named for Effie Jewell, the first child born in the developing coal camp in the early 1900s. Sometimes the name has been attributed to the "jewels" of coal in the rich mountain seams, but Dorothy Cook, in a 1988 interview in the local magazine *Blackberry Winter*, verified the naming of the town for its first newborn. (Courtesy of Mary Elizabeth Jewell Henderson.)

Willie O. White (1905–1998) was in the grocery business at Jewell Ridge from 1944 until 1986. Patrons knew they could find "almost everything" in her store. She is remembered as being proud for having the coldest Cokes on the mountain during the hot summer days. (Courtesy of Ginger Mustard.)

Amie Lee Allen Mullins (left) and Jess Mullins lived in Jewell Ridge and Chicken Ridge for 44 years. With them is their granddaughter Jessceah (sic) Stewart. Jess worked in the mines until 1950. After that time, he operated a truck mine and provided ponies for the coal company for four additional years. (Courtesy of Lynda Mayhorn.)

Robert Bowman (left) and Roy Lee Smith were among the many young men who left Jewell Ridge to join the military. Patriotism was felt in the community and in the work place, and was emphasized by the officers of the coal company. Awards for mine and community achievements were often in the form of savings bonds. (Courtesy of Harry David Taylor.)

On a summer day in 1957, Katherine Richardson poses with her children. She is holding baby Mary Katherine, and standing in front are (from left to right) Mike, Bill, and Sandy. (Courtesy of Katherine Richardson.)

Lucille Fox plays with her grandson Jeff Martin at the Fox home on the "Spur." They are in the yard of the log house just outside of Jewell Ridge in 1948. Jeff's grandfather is George Fox. (Courtesy of Elizabeth Fox Martin.)

Ed and Juanita Gilbert stand in front of their Jewell Ridge home. Among the servicemen who were pictured in the January 1944 edition of the *Jewell Journal* was a member of the Gilbert family, Pfc. John E. Gilbert, who was serving overseas along with many other patriotic Jewell Ridge residents. (Courtesy of John Gilbert.)

John Rufus Smith was a respected Tazewell County deputy and a community and political leader in the Jewell Ridge area. In 1936, he was gunned down in the road in front of his house on Smith Ridge in a random act of violence. His funeral drew one of the largest crowds remembered in the region. (Courtesy of Katherine Richardson.)

Ed Gilbert (left) and his son John were members of another family who were original settlers at Jewell Ridge. They are pictured here in 1967. Bliss Gilbert, brother of Ed, lived in the center of town in earlier days and raised a large family. (Courtesy of John Gilbert.)

Miners have always been a proud and industrious clan. Here is Ed Gilbert in his work clothes, holding his dinner pail. Workers in Jewell Ridge—other than the miners—included employees of the company store. Store managers were George Day and E. J. Huddleston, among others. Workers who held different positions in the company store included Paul Hefner, Butch Reedy, John McClintock, George Kennedy, Hobe Morgan, "Ma" Sanders, Melvin VanDyke, Bane VanDyke, Henry Elswick, Lexie M. Kennedy, and C. N. Petty. (Courtesy of John Gilbert.)

Two

HOME ON THE RIDGE

Among the buildings constructed in the new town was the clubhouse. It was probably one of the most used buildings in the community. Thirteen unidentified workmen can be seen on the roof. (Courtesy of John McClintock Jr.)

The winding road up the mountain to Jewell Ridge was picturesque, but in winter weather, it was treacherous. The camp was sometimes isolated from the rest of the county in the days before the road was paved and automobiles climbed up the mountain. There are still residents of Jewell Ridge who remember navigating the winding road on foot or on horseback. Tipple Hill is remembered as the steepest place along the town road, especially when school buses made the daily journey. (Courtesy of Gaynelle Thompson.)

The center of Jewell Ridge in the late 1930s and early 1940s was a good place to live. On the right is the clubhouse, which was operated for many years by Samantha Christian and her husband, A. M. "Doc" Christian. At one time there were 30 boarders living at the clubhouse. Samantha Christian also fed the teachers at the Jewell Ridge School and the patients at the hospital. (Courtesy of Margaret Matney.)

The YMCA, Presbyterian church, the water tower, and part of the store were in the center of the coal camp before the disastrous fire destroyed many of the buildings. Before 1936, the roads were not paved and the rock walls had not been built. After the fire, the coal company built new, stronger, and more modern buildings. The YMCA, built in 1926 for the entertainment of the miners and officials, featured a theater that showed the latest silent films. The YMCA building housed not only the movie theater, but also a pool hall, soda fountain, snack bar, post office, and barbershop. It was managed by John W. McClintock Sr. During the 1936 fire, the YMCA building was dynamited to keep the flames from spreading to the rest of the camp. (Courtesy of Margaret Matney.)

The clubhouse, a large structure, was not only a hotel, but also was a gathering place for the community. Pictured in front of the clubhouse are (from left to right) Stella Christian, Jean Joyce, Samantha Christian, and four unidentified. Jewell Ridge residents of the early days of mine production appreciated their unique town on top of the ridge. After World War II, when the coal production slowed, the camp did not become a forgotten ghost town. Many of the houses were sold to individuals, the descendants of the first miners, and they have been kept in the excellent condition envisioned by George W. St. Clair. (Courtesy of Margaret Matney.)

The YMCA was an ornate building and one of the biggest the coal company built. It is believed to be the first YMCA complex in Tazewell County. The building housed a theater, a poolroom, a post office, a library, and a barbershop. John Terry, Bob Jessee, and Clarence Shaw were popular barbers. Postmasters at Jewell Ridge, between 1928 and 1971, were Oscar Elswick, Henry H. Elswick, Bernard B. Mahood, Lexie M. Kennedy, Eliza B. Kennedy, Earl T. Patton, and Mary G. Bush. After the 1936 fire, the new company store was erected on the YMCA site. (Courtesy of Margaret Matney.)

Jewell Ridge in the late evening looks peaceful as night creeps into the ridge. Among the conversation of all newcomers to Jewell Ridge has always been the beauty of the seasons and the spectacular sunrises and sunsets that can be seen from the elevation of 3,500 feet. This picture shows the area below the store with Newtown in the distance. (Courtesy of Margaret Matney.)

The clubhouse (left) and the school (later the hospital) are pictured here soon after the trees were planted. In the original plans for the town, George W. St. Clair emphasized the planting of trees at every house and business. The location was surrounded by natural timber when the building took place, and much of it remains intact. (Courtesy of Margaret Matney.)

The mine superintendent's home is surrounded by one of the beautiful stone walls that can be found throughout the coal camp. One of the early superintendents was James A. Hagy, who moved to Jewell Ridge in 1942. The first coal corporation was incorporated in 1910 with George W. St. Clair and Thomas M. Righter as partners. Later the following officers are listed: George W. St. Clair, president; Huston St. Clair, vice president in charge of operations; Robert H. Moore, treasurer; C. R. Brown, secretary; and T. T. Rees, general superintendent. (Courtesy of Margaret Matney.)

The photographer must have understood the community spirit of Jewell Ridge when he included the following caption along with the typical street scene: "Neat houses and neighbors who care is a hallmark of the closeness of growing up in Jewell Ridge." (Courtesy of Harry David Taylor.)

The porch at the clubhouse looks inviting, as it must have been for the early boarders who came to Jewell Ridge. This hotel served as temporary housing for a myriad of visitors who made their way to the top of the mountain. (Courtesy of Gaynelle Thompson.)

The first houses on top of the ridge, built for the employees of the Jewell Ridge Coal Corporation by George W. St. Clair, were comfortable with neat yards that had paling fences and young trees. The main road through the community was paved as soon as automobiles became common. (Courtesy of Gaynelle Thompson.)

The long stone walls around the Jewell Ridge Park and at other town locations are a beautiful asset always noticed by visitors. The coal company office and the store can be seen in the background. The trees were planted as part of the overall plan of George W. St. Clair to build the model town. (Courtesy of Margaret Matney.)

The C. R. Burke home is especially beautiful on a day of snow. The Burkes were a pioneering family on the ridge, and through the years, they have been connected with the mining operation and with farming. The Burke family exemplifies this description from the *Coal People* magazine in 1987: "The coal industry's distinctive culture creates strong bonds which tie people together. Their memories are among the industry's greatest treasures." (Courtesy of Bill Patton.)

The smokehouse at the M. M. Burke home was built in the 1930s. The early Burke family had large land holdings in the Jewell Ridge area. James C. Burke was the first store manager of the commissary owned by the Jewell Ridge Coal Corporation. Mathes Burke operated a dairy and sold milk products to the stores at Jewell Ridge and Jewell Valley. (Courtesy of Carol Mullins.)

This is the home of Whitten Joyce and his family. It is one of the many beautiful homes at Jewell Ridge. When George W. St. Clair built the town, high above the mining operation, he spared no expense. The original town consisted of 105 white houses with slate-shingled roofs. They were arranged in two rows on the top of the ridge. The community was known for its neat and clean houses and streets. (Courtesy of Loraine Johnson.)

Three

WORK ON THE RIDGE

Dr. Huston St. Clair (left) succeeded his father, George W. St. Clair, as president of the Jewell Ridge Coal Corporation. Pictured with him is H. D. "Hump" Smith, mine superintendent. Dr. St. Clair was a medical doctor who went into the coal business with his father after an accident prevented him from actively practicing medicine. He served as the 1942–1944 president of the Virginia Chamber of Commerce, where he gained wide recognition for his promotion of Virginia educational opportunities. (Courtesy of Jewell Ridge Archives.)

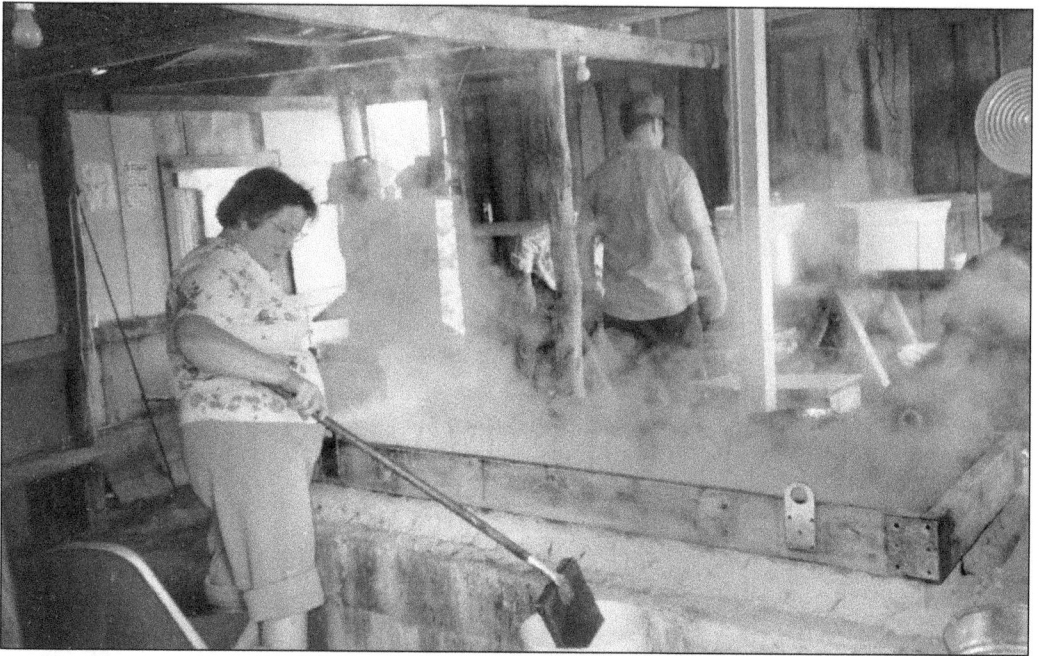

Juanita Cook Deskins (left) skims the foam from molasses made in Jewell Ridge in recent years. She follows a tradition established when the mountains and valleys of Southwest Virginia had large fields of cane and most families had biscuits and molasses for breakfast on cold winter mornings. Homer Nelson (standing in the background) assists in the task. (Courtesy of Carol Mullins.)

Clarence "Preach" Alicie tests the cane molasses to see if it is ready for consumption. Along with the molasses and hot biscuits, Jewell Ridge cooks are known for other good food and their hospitality to friends and strangers. In the early days of the coal-mining era, many women made cakes and pies, and sold them at the commissary for extra income. (Courtesy of Carol Mullins.)

The first tipple at the new Jewell Ridge mine was constructed in 1905. In 1935, a modern steel tipple was erected. Norfolk and Western Railway coal cars have, through the years, carried the rich coal out of the mountains. Jewell Ridge coal was famed for its high metallurgical qualities, as well as its low ash and low sulphur. It was always in wide demand by the steel industry. A 1931 history records 2,000 tons of coal dumped daily into a tipple located about one-half mile from the mine. (Courtesy of Barbara Altizer and Robert Moore.)

The belt line built inside the Jewell Ridge mine in 1945 was a great safety addition to the mining operation, as well as a time saver. The huge conveyors carried coal directly to the tipples. Also in the 1940s, the giant Jeffrey Centrifugal fan was installed to modernize the overall ventilating system in the mines. At that time, the fan furnished fresh air to 200 workers on the day shift and 50 workers on the night shift. (Courtesy of Jewell Ridge Recreation Department.)

Charlie Walker and John McVey check some of the thousands of records stored in the company office. Included were payroll and wage records, as well as the inventory of business transactions necessary to operate the successful coal enterprise. (Courtesy of Jewell Ridge Archives.)

The company store at Jewell Ridge (and other communities) was a community meeting place, as well as a place to purchase all necessities. Local historian Harry David Taylor described the store: "The old company store had a fragrance. Sometimes you could get a whiff of vanilla, a touch of coffee, some oranges, cabbage, chocolate, molasses, fertilizer, onions, leather, and that unidentifiable perfume that reminded one of baby powder. The dry-goods department smelled like new overalls and dresses that had just been ironed. Sometimes Ivory or Lifebuoy soap, or a cigar or lamp oil would invade your senses." George Day was the store manager. (Courtesy of Barbara Altizer and Robert Moore.)

The company store, pictured here perhaps during the Christmas season, appealed to all ages. After the 1936 fire and the building of the new store, E. J. Huddleston was the manager, with Paul Hefner as his assistant. Hefner is pictured on the left with a group of unidentified customers. Lester "Butch" Reedy was the store butcher. John McClintock took care of the candy, tobacco, and sundries. George Kennedy was in charge of grocery checkout, and Hobe Morgan was in charge of delivery. Melvin VanDyke oversaw maintenance and the bowling alley. Bane VanDyke took care of the filling station. Most of the customers used the company-issued scrip to make purchases. (Courtesy of Jewell Ridge Archives.)

Dr. Rufus Brittain was a revered Jewell Ridge doctor—one of many who practiced medicine in the community hospital—who delivered babies (many named Rufus) and dispensed practical wisdom that endeared him to his patients. Dr. A. M. Larghey was one of the first doctors, and he insisted that the boy babies he delivered carry the name of "Harry." Also well remembered are Dr. L. R. McCormack and his assistant, Delores Mulkey. (Courtesy of Margaret Matney.)

One of the nurses who served in the Jewell Ridge Hospital was ? Bailey. She is standing on the clubhouse steps. Another nurse who is well remembered was ? Glienke, who worked for many years with Dr. Rufus Brittain. When World War II was declared, she returned to her home in Germany. The nurses were an integral part of Jewell Ridge, serving well beyond their duties. (Courtesy of Margaret Matney.)

A. M. Christian (left) and his unknown companion helped build the houses at Jewell Ridge in the 1920s. Two brothers, Clarence and Millard Farmer, came to the ridge shortly after the disastrous 1936 fire and helped rebuild the store. In September 1936, a fire destroyed the company store, the YMCA, theater, library, and the church. As a last-ditch effort, a portion of the YMCA building was dynamited to keep the fire from spreading into the row of houses. New buildings soon took shape, and it was spread throughout the area that Jewell Ridge would again stand on the high ridges, proud and strong. (Courtesy of Margaret Matney.)

Visiting before going to work are (from left to right) Roby Wysong (foreman of the mine machine shop), ? Wilson, A. M. Christian, and (front) ? Glienke, hospital nurse. Many of the community workers and the miners who did not choose to relocate their families on the ridge stayed at the clubhouse. According to Ruby Smith, a longtime resident of Jewell Ridge, "Tenants were provided with two cooked meals a day, and their lunches were packed." The early doctor and dentist offices were in the clubhouse, too. A. M. and Samantha Christian were in charge of the clubhouse for many years. (Courtesy of Margaret Matney.)

Thomas and Rachel Altizer carried on the Jewell Ridge tradition of serving delicious food. The early settlers raised most of their food in large gardens that covered the steep mountains and fertile valleys. The Altizer family has deep family roots in the area, and Thomas and Rachel were likely among those described by Harry David Taylor as "miners and farmers, both important jobs. In the early spring a pungent smoke filled the air as plots were cleared, weeds were burned, and the jangle of trace chains made happy sounds as horses turned the earth." (Courtesy of Margaret Matney.)

This group poses on a day in spring. Pictured from left to right are Thomas Altizer, Rachel Christian Altizer, Myrtle Christian, Samantha Ward Christian, John Christian, Carl Altizer, and A. M. "Doc" Christian. Doc was one of the men who helped put in the mine drift mouth, and his wife ran the clubhouse at Jewell Ridge for many years. Boarders at the clubhouse included teachers, deputy sheriffs, some miners, salesmen, and visiting dignitaries. (Courtesy of Margaret Matney.)

Pierce Elswick takes a breather from his work in the mine. Note the shovel he uses to load coal and the kneepads he uses to protect his legs. The support used to hold up the roof is known as a "timber," and it is held against the top with a header and a wedge. (Courtesy of Jewell Ridge Archives.)

The maintenance crew works on the mining equipment and tracks. Both were carefully guarded and well cared for. In fact, during the time of the Jewell Ridge operation, this mine was considered state-of-the-art. The Jewell Ridge miners took pride in both their facilities and their accomplishments. (Courtesy of Jewell Ridge Archives.)

The work of the Jewell Ridge miner was not easy. With the advent of modern mining machinery, the job became somewhat less taxing, but the miner's work continued to be a difficult undertaking. Nevertheless, the Jewell Ridge mine continued to produce massive tonnage of coal well into the 20th century. (Courtesy of Jewell Ridge Archives.)

A group of Jewell Ridge employees are pictured near the mining operation. The men seem to be enjoying a rare moment of relaxation at their place of work. Coal miners and mining engineers appear to have come together for this joint photo opportunity. (Courtesy of Jewell Ridge Archives.)

Beau Duncan (left) and Howard Miller enjoy a break in the office routine. The Jewell Ridge office personnel kept meticulous records. An example of the pay envelope issued to each employee of the mine belonged to J. H. Taylor in August 1953. It reads, "72 and ½ hours work $175.20. Doctor $1.25. Bath $1.50. Tax $15.23. Total $159.22." (Courtesy of Harry David Taylor.)

A cutting machine shears through the "face" of the coal, the point at which the miners are working. The coal was then loaded into cars or shoveled onto a conveyor belt. Even with modern equipment, the work of the coal miner was difficult. In addition, the use of modern mining machinery demanded continual awareness of potential dangers in all mining operations. (Courtesy of Jewell Ridge Archives.)

The deep recesses of the earth held the famous Jewell Ridge coal, recognized for its excellence around the world. The mining operation no longer exists, but the town of Jewell Ridge is a viable community with great memories and an optimistic outlook on the days to come. (Courtesy of Jewell Ridge Archives.)

This trip of coal cars is on the way to the tipple to be dumped. There the slate would be removed by slate pickers. Then the coal was graded by size, was cleaned, and was loaded into rail gondolas. Finally, the black gold was delivered by the Norfolk and Western Railway to distant points. (Courtesy of Jewell Ridge Archives.)

The unidentified miner pictured here is drilling a hole in the side of the mine with a hand-cranked breast auger. The holes were bored in the mine seam for blasting. After the blast, the coal was on its way for final preparation. (Courtesy of Jewell Ridge Archives.)

This building was a modern structure used for the Jewell Ridge operations payroll department. It was simultaneously used as the company store. As a result, this edifice and the two businesses it housed were of extreme importance to the entire Jewell Ridge community. (Courtesy of Jewell Ridge Archives.)

Engineers C. P. Howard and Charles Hoover test new equipment installed to dump coal by flipping the mining cars completely over. The Jewell Ridge mining operations was recognized for always having the latest, most modern equipment. Safety was an important goal on every shift. (Courtesy of Jewell Ridge Archives.)

The engineering department at Jewell Ridge had a variety of tasks. The blueprints and layouts for the underground mining operation were meticulously drawn and copied. From left to right, Johnny Tizen, Stewart Kennedy, C. P. Howard, and Charles Hoover pause from the work before them. (Courtesy of Jewell Ridge Archives.)

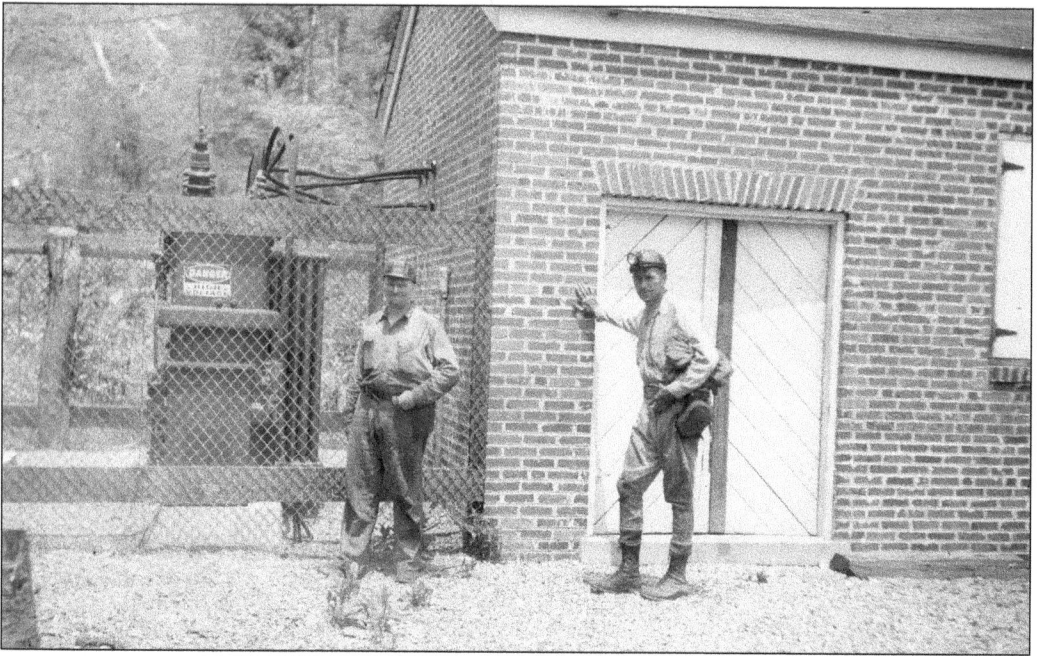

Two of the "movers and shakers" in the Jewell Ridge coal operations were James Hagy (left) and Humphrey "Hump" Smith. Hagy was a mine superintendent, and Smith was a general manager. The Hagy and Smith families were among the early settlers in the Jewell Ridge area. (Courtesy of Jewell Ridge Archives.)

This miner is tending a belt line as the coal is conveyed into a mining coal car. At the time, this was an innovation in the coal loader operations of the Jewell Ridge mine. Loading coal became an easier task with the use of the conveyor belt line. (Courtesy of Jewell Ridge Archives.)

Thomas Lester Cox (seated) and his son John Ralph Cox, operators of the Cox Lumber Company, cleared large tracts of timber in the 1940s and 1950s from the Jewell Ridge and Jewell Valley areas. An earlier timbering operation in the same area was managed by Chapman Chambers. (Courtesy of Delores Cox Blankenship.)

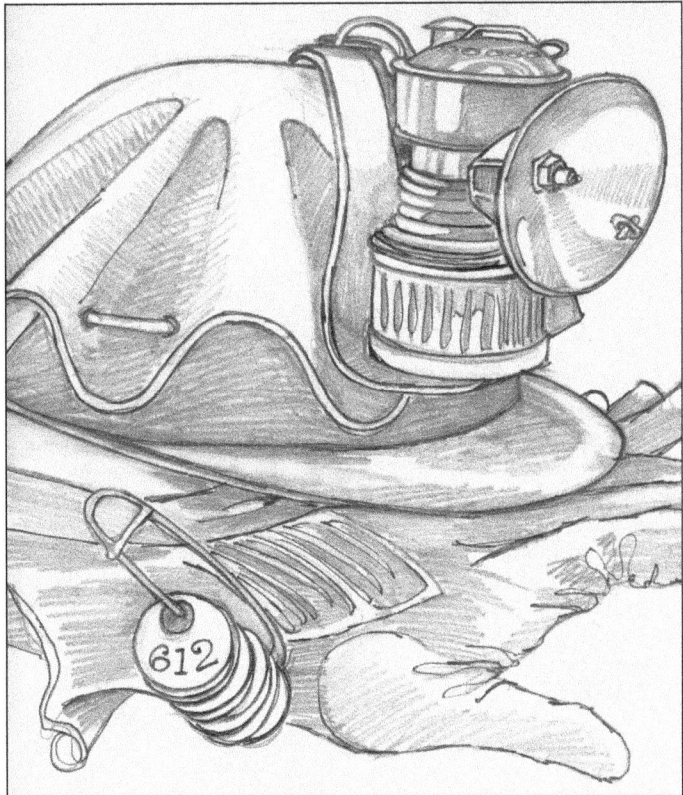

The early coal miner's tools, the lifeblood of Jewell Ridge, are depicted here by Ellen Elmes in her artistic work, emphasizing the area coal industry. Included is the miner's carbide lamp on his cap and the numbered metal "checks" that marked the coal loader's identity. (Courtesy of Ellen Elmes.)

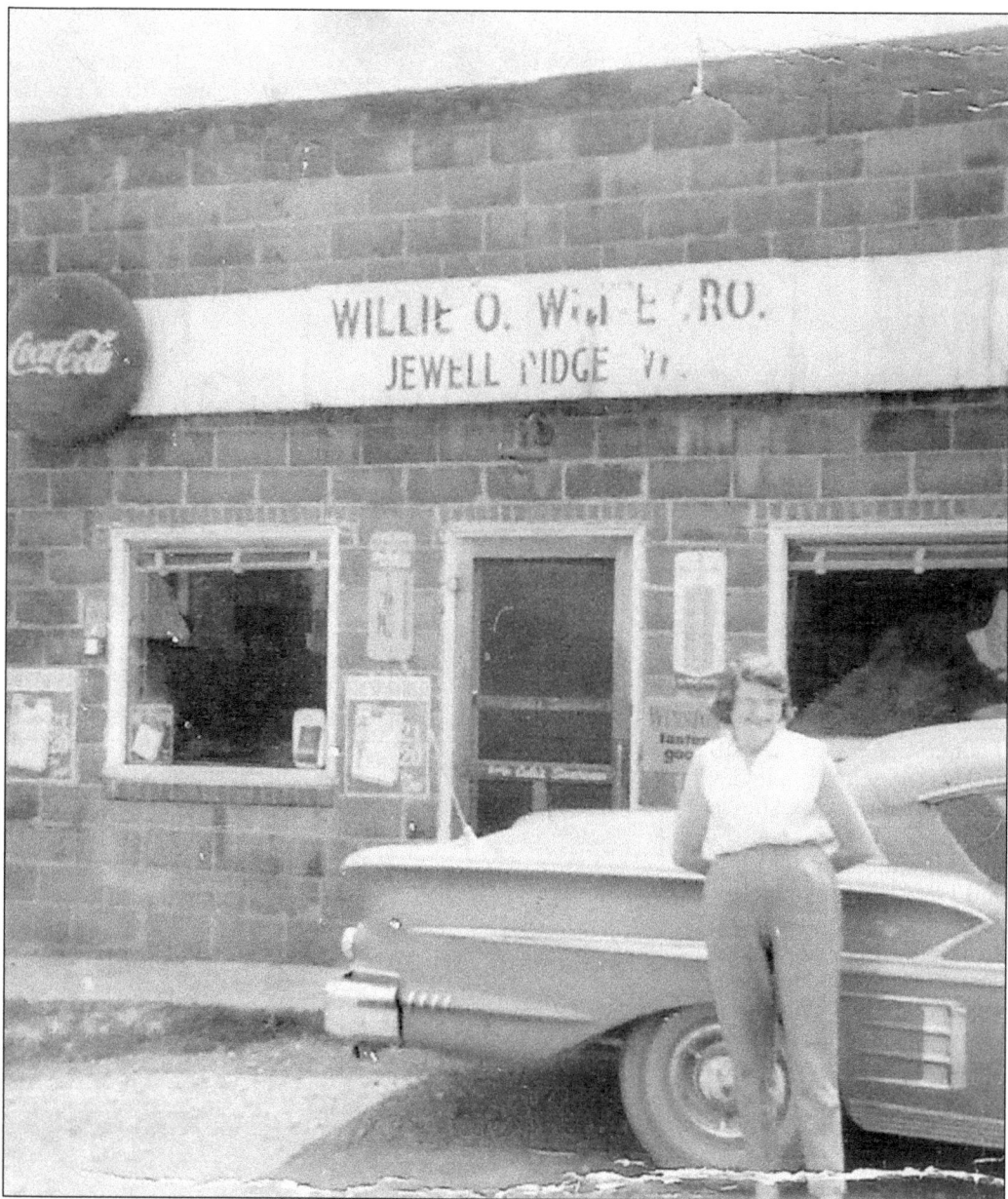

Willie O. White looks ready to welcome customers to her Jewell Ridge business, which she operated for more than 40 years. The stores on the ridges were always well stocked, starting with the company store operated by the mining company. In the first years of the camp, before good roads and cars, materials were brought up the mountain by a hoist or cable car built by the coal company. (Courtesy of Ginger Mustard.)

Perry Farmer White was instrumental in the formation of the UMWA No. 7068 at Jewell Ridge and served as the local president. In 1938, he traveled to Washington, D.C., and Pittsburgh, Pennsylvania, on union business and met the famous John L. Lewis. White lost his right leg in a mining accident when he was 17. Because of this accident, he was aware of the safety needs in the industry and worked tirelessly for the rights of the underground coal miners. The man pictured on the left is unknown. (Courtesy of Ginger Mustard.)

The water storage tank at the Jewell Ridge mining operation stood above the tipple. On this day, coal was being loaded on the Norfolk and Western Railway cars bound for worldwide distribution. (Courtesy of Jewell Ridge Archives.)

Postmaster Oscar Elswick was one of the first postmasters who served the Jewell Ridge community. The daily mail service was important to the mining operation and to the families who lived on and near the ridge. An early post office was located in the YMCA building. (Courtesy of Harry David Taylor.)

The *Jewell Journal* was published by the coal company for many years and was especially valuable for Jewell Ridge families during the years of World War II, when the news of local servicemen was given a special page. Jewell Ridge was required to observe blackout regulations during World War II due to the community's high elevation. The newspaper was printed in Tazewell by the *Clinch Valley News*. George W .St. Clair edited the first editions, and then he turned the editorship over to J. Howard Miller and his assistant, C. M. Brown. (Courtesy of Harry David Taylor.)

Earl Patton (left) and Mildred Burke Patton were both affiliated with the Jewell Ridge post office. Earl Patton was postmaster in 1968 and 1969. Mildred Patton was postal clerk from 1970 to 1985. The first Jewell Ridge postmaster was Henry H. Elswick, who assumed the office in December 1928. (Courtesy of Bill Patton.)

Winters can be cold at Jewell Ridge's high elevation. In 1970, when photographer Bill Patton took this picture, the water tank resembled a dripping ice cream cone. Patton is a descendant of a pioneer Jewell Ridge family who probably, through the years, saw many picturesque winter scenes—frigid but beautiful. (Courtesy of Bill Patton.)

State mine inspectors John Keene and Alex St. Clair worked at the mines in 1958. Keene (left) demonstrates the hand-cranked breast auger that was used in early mining to drill bore holes into the coal seam for blasting. St. Clair (right) holds the pick. The safety of the mining operation was always a top priority of the owners. (Courtesy of William P. Keene.)

Margaret Catherine (left) and Charles Wesley Hylton ran the Jewell Ridge boardinghouse in the early days, when single miners, salesmen, and sometimes teachers had accommodations there. The Hyltons were often called "Grandpa and Grandma." (Courtesy of Katherine Richardson.)

Four prominent engineers with the Jewell Ridge Coal Corporation were (seated) Alex Richardson; (second row, from left to right) Clint Nearhood and C. P. Howard; (third row) Nancy Bowman, wife of D. L. Bowman. (Courtesy of Katherine Smith Richardson.)

The open spaces in the center of the Jewell Ridge community were one of the attractions of the model coal camp. Young trees and flowering shrubs outline the lush, green, town center and exemplify the pride that the residents of the community and the coal company officials shared in their mountaintop setting. (Courtesy of Barbara Altizer and Robert Moore.)

Jewell Ridge in its summer beauty deserves the praise written in 1927 by Madison A. Dunlap, a nationally recognized leader in coal operations, following a visit to the Tazewell County corporation. It reads: "Tazewell County is entitled to be justly proud of so great an achievement, lifting the

84

ordinary dirty business of coal mining from the grime and gloom of the valleys up to a village of cleanliness and beauty, sparkling in the sunlight up above the world so high." Indeed Jewell Ridge was that diamond in Tazewell County's sky. (Courtesy of Grubb Photo and Robert Moore.)

The realistic pick and shovel sketched by Ellen Elmes represent important tools used by the first miners who worked at Jewell Ridge. Tons of valuable coal were removed with these tools, wielded by dedicated underground workers. The typical miner's pick was sharp on both ends. The shovel was commonly called a "number four red-edge." (Courtesy of Ellen Elmes.)

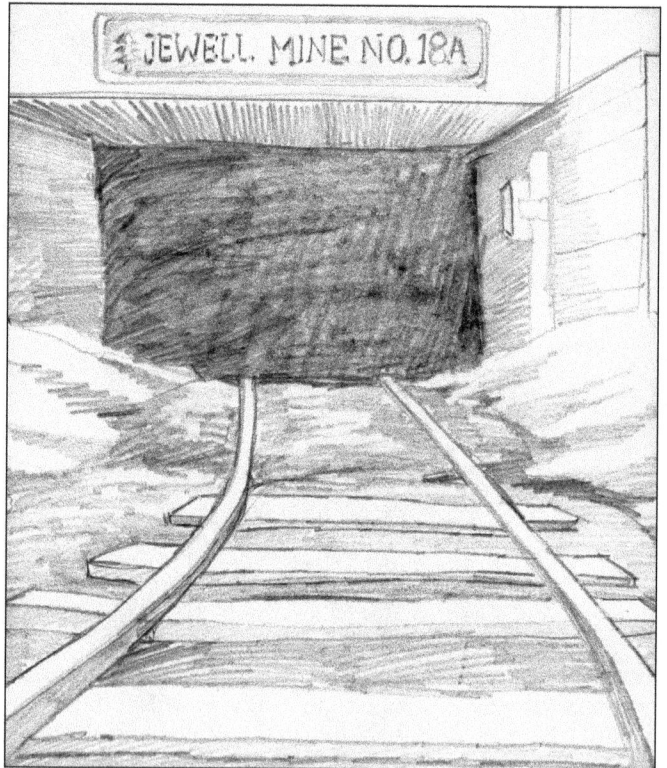

The portal, "drift mouth," of Jewell Mine No. 18A is depicted here by artist Ellen Elmes. She is retired from the faculty at Southwest Virginia Community College (SVCC), where she taught and advised students for many years as an art professor. (Courtesy of Ellen Elmes.)

Symbols of mining at the Jewell Ridge coal mine were often illustrative of the most modern images available during the years of the Jewell Ridge Coal Corporation's existence. This depiction by Ellen Elmes is an example of the early coal-mining experience. In the background is a $1 piece of scrip. In the foreground, symbols of the miner's workday include the mining car and the miner's lunch pail. (Courtesy of Ellen Elmes.)

Ellen Elmes, a historical mural painter and resident of the Jewell Ridge community, created a mural emphasizing the coal industry for the engineering building at Southwest Virginia Community College (SVCC). The center section of the canvas shows Jewell Ridge with the YMCA; the clubhouse (left); and the tipple (right), which was originally below the ridge. The men above the buildings are (from left to right) O. P. Allen, a contractor; Dr. Rufus Brittain, a Jewell Ridge doctor; and George W. St. Clair, founder and president of the Jewell Ridge Coal Corporation. Don Elmes photographed the mural in Davis Hall on the SVCC campus. (Courtesy of Ellen Elmes and Don Elmes.)

Four

STUDY ON THE RIDGE

The school and playground in the town of Jewell Ridge is pictured here in the early 1920s and described by John McClintock Jr. This school building was later converted into the hospital run by Dr. Rufus Brittain. There must have been a carnival at the Jewell Ridge School on this day for all these people to enjoy, including a maypole to the right. (Courtesy of Gaynelle Thompson.)

Boyd B. Burdette was principal of the Jewell Ridge School in 1938. He is pictured with his wife, Naomi Brewster Burdette (right), and his daughter Patricia (center) The Jewell Ridge Coal Corporation provided excellent elementary schools and recruited quality teachers, who were given an extra stipend by the coal company in addition to their county salary. Many teachers married Jewell Ridge men and spent the rest of their lives on the mountaintop. (Courtesy of Carol Mullins.)

A great unifying force at Jewell Ridge has always been the church. Seated on the steps of the Presbyterian church in 1945 with the minister, Manson B. Tate, are some of the schoolteachers, who were also prominent as church leaders. They are, from left to right, Helen Creasy, Manson B. Tate, ? Collins, Betty Kyle Barnett, Pearl Breckenridge Nipper, Gladys Nester, Clara Scott, and Elizabeth Fox. (Courtesy of Carol Mullins.)

Jewell Ridge high school students attended Richlands High School, and in 1949, these students worked together at the Richlands library before catching the school bus up the ridge. They are (from left to right) Barbara Cook Stevens, unidentified, Sonny Gear, Doris Bowman, Peggy Taylor Elliott, Harold Keene, and Charles "Coonie" Blankenship. (Courtesy of Carol Mullins.)

The seventh-grade teacher and principal at the Jewell Ridge School in 1947 was Clara Scott. Her students that year were, from left to right, (first row) Patricia Nearhood, Jean Jewel, Christina Shell, Edna Goss, Jacquelyn Overstreet, Jean Blankenship, Gretta Blankenship, and Janet Wilson; (second row) Bobbie Ann Kiser, Thelma Johnson, Ann Lewis, Deloris Regan, Betty Breckenridge, Helen Draughan, Gaynelle Sullivan, Earl Young, Anna Lenhart, Lucian Woosley, Earl Jewell, and Harold Childress; (third row) Carol Cook, Peggy Rhea, Mary Alice Whited, Junior Keen, Gray Edwards, and Steward Smith; (fourth row) Bobby Lee VanDyke, Thomas Shelton, Noel Stallard, David Jessee, Estil Smith, unidentified, and Corbin "Tubby" Hawkins. (Courtesy of Carol Mullins.)

The Jewell Ridge Presbyterian Bible School in 1952 had about 120 children and teachers in attendance. Those who attended could identify only a few in the picture. In no particular order, they include Dusty Gess, Johnny Smith, Buddy Smith, Jimmy Kennedy, Susie Barnette, John Gess, Ronnie VanDyke, Benson Bell, Jenny Lynn Kennedy, Charlotte Gilbert, Sonny Farmer, Mary Helen Sullivan, Scotty Arrington, Jerry Blanton, Dan Stout, Flora Barnette, Deloris Regan, Ollie Jean Blanton, Phyllis Blankenship, Blanch Penny, Jimmy Smith, Teddy Hess, Carol Keen, Margaret Ketchum, Wilma Whittaker, and Mary Coker. (Courtesy of Carol Mullins.)

In 1930, this group was photographed on the porch of the old school at Jewell Ridge. They are, from left to right, as follows: (first row) Stanley Smith, Alexander Marion " Doc" Christian, Dorothy Scott (church secretary), and Nancy Smith; (second row) M. M .Burke, Belle Burke, Edna VanDyke, R. T. L. Liston (Presbyterian minister), and Frank Zeigler (coal company superintendent). At one time, every separate ridge had a one- or two-room school. Eventually, they consolidated into the Jewell Ridge School, which went to the seventh grade. In the late 1960s, the new Jewell Ridge Elementary School was built, and it served the community until closing in 1996. (Courtesy of Carol Mullins.)

Dr. T. A. Freeman, minister at the Jewell Ridge Presbyterian Church, was a friend to people of every age, and he is remembered today with fondness. Some of the other ministers who served the religious needs of the miners and their families include John Brown, Manson Tate, Paul Gess, John Parks, Bert Edwards, Ben Brown, Arthur S. Gear, Hugh D. R. Pollard, Sidney Anderson, Hazel Berry, Elmon Brown, and Richard Stone. Dr. Freeman is standing on the steps of the M. M. Burke home. (Courtesy of Carol Mullins.)

Community gatherings, such as the one pictured here, were the highlight of the calendar on the ridge. Here residents gather for a big celebration honoring the Reverend Dr. W. W. Arrowood, a Presbyterian minister, in the school's gymnasium. To the right is John Culbertson, Jewell Ridge School principal. (Courtesy of Jewell Ridge Archives.)

An appreciation celebration for the teachers at Jewell Ridge brought out a full house of parents. The six teachers are (from left to right) Elizabeth Crenshaw, Kay Harris, Gaye Harris, Kate Taylor, Clara Scott, and Helen Creasy. Howard "Bud" Miller (seated, center) was president of the Parent-Teacher Association, the sponsor of the event. (Courtesy of Jewell Ridge Archives.)

A bright and happy group of students in Helen Creasy's class stops long enough for Howard "Bud" Miller to take their picture. Included, but not in any particular order, are Ann Lewis, Patricia Nearhood, Gaynelle Sullivan, Delores Regan, Carol Cook, Christine Shell, Peggy Rhea, Lucille Jessee, Jean Jewell, Thelma Johnson, Lucille Gilbert, Jacqueline Overstreet, Edna Goss, and Bobby Lee VanDyke. Note the appropriate sign on the left wall above the display: "What bituminous coal has done for man." (Courtesy of Jewell Ridge Archives.)

The Jewell Ridge Parent-Teacher Association sponsored an annual school carnival. Hundreds of students and adults enjoyed the grand event. This carnival in the 1940s honored Nick Miller as king and Peggy Howard as queen. Other carnival attendees included (in no particular order) Johnny Barnette, Elizabeth Crenshaw, Helen Crenshaw, Kenneth Smith, Robert Rumgay, Janet Wilson and Peggy Smith. (Courtesy of Jewell Ridge Archives.)

A Bible school class of boys at the Presbyterian church included, from left to right, the following: (first row) Douglas White, Don Shelton, Harold Edwards, and ? Palmer; (second row) David Burke, Ralph Brown, Eugene Buchanan, Howard McCoy, Ralph Johnson, and ? Palmer. (Courtesy of Jewell Ridge Archives.)

In March 1942, Dr. Huston St. Clair presented a check for $3,995.01 to Josh Keene, president of the employee's burial fund association. This amount represented the savings in compensation costs at the mine for the last eight months of 1942. Speakers at the occasion were J. A. Hagy, mine superintendent, and W. H. Tomlinson, district engineer for the Bureau of Mines. They commended the miners for their safety record. (Courtesy of Jewell Ridge Archives.)

Eunice Lewis (left) presents an award to her fellow teacher, Elizabeth Crenshaw. They taught in the Jewell Ridge Elementary School in the mid-1940s. The ceremony and reception were sponsored by the Parent-Teacher Association. (Courtesy of Jewell Ridge Archives.)

Harry David Taylor is pictured in front of the church with his Bible school class. Summer Bible schools were often conducted by the public school teachers who stayed in Jewell Ridge during their summer vacations. Only three of these students are identified. They are Nick Miller (with tie), Jackie (left), and Phyllis Blankenship (standing to the right of Taylor). (Courtesy of Jewell Ridge Archives.)

A group of Girl Scouts is pictured in front of the Jewell Ridge Coal Corporation bus. The group poses as the members prepare to descend the ridge for a summer adventure. Girl Scout camp was often held at Camp Sequoia near Sullins College in Bristol. Pictured from left to right are the following: (first row) Doris Bowman, Gladys Nester, Ann Lewis, Phyllis Jessee, Peggy Vance, two unidentified, Bobby Ann Kiser, and Betty Breckenridge; (second row) Barbara Cook, two unidentified, Evelyn Buchanan, Betty Rhea, and Carol Cook. The young people of Jewell Ridge often left their community for educational opportunities throughout the region. (Courtesy of Jewell Ridge Archives.)

These students at the Jewell Ridge School in 1937 cannot all be named. Some of those attending school that year included (not in order) David Reed, Rudolph Taylor, Mable Burgess, Imogene Reedy, Margaret Joyce, and Tommy Patteson. Education was an important part of the life of Jewell Ridge families. The coal company supplemented the salary of teachers who stayed at Jewell Ridge through the summer months to help with church programs and recreational activities. (Courtesy of Margaret Matney.)

Jewell Ridge teachers lived in a "teacherage" provided by the coal company for many years. Teachers pictured are (from left to right) Emily Kemp, Stella Christian, Boyd "Red" Burdett, Mary Brown, Alice Orr, and Gwendolyn Humphry. Dorothy Cook, in an interview for the local magazine *Blackberry Winters*, described the first schools: "When the school was built, they had two rooms with two teachers . . . You studied reading, writing and arithmetic. When you learned it, you graduated to the next grade. You started when you were six years old." (Courtesy of Margaret Matney.)

In 1938, Alma Stallard taught this children's Sunday school class. She is pictured at the top, to the left. Seated, from top to bottom and left to right, are Phyllis Jessee, Jerry Austen, three unidentified, Jimmy Joyce, unidentified, Paul E. Cook, unidentified, David Czokas, unidentified, ? Brown, two unidentified, Mary Shelton, and two unidentified. (Courtesy of Margaret Matney.)

The annual homecoming celebration draws many Jewell Ridgers home. This group was pictured at one of those homecomings. From left to right are Ann Shortridge, Edith Joyce Hanna, Letha Ratliff, Jackie Ratliff Fletcher, and Gladys Christian Joyce. From the early days, active Scouting programs, garden clubs, Parent-Teacher Associations, youth groups at school and church, and recreational activities have been promoted, particularly when the well-known recreation director Clark M. Brown came to the ridge in 1942. (Courtesy of Margaret Matney.)

The Jewell Ridge Presbyterian Church remains a unifying force, and the ministers who have served through the years have each helped in the town's development. The first church was destroyed in the 1936 fire when Dr. T. A. Freeman was the leader. George W. St. Clair was a devoted worker in the Presbyterian Church, both in Tazewell and Jewell Ridge, and his strong influence was felt in the town and in the workplace. The current interim pastor at the church is William P. Keene. (Courtesy of Margaret Matney.)

A recent Presbyterian minister in Jewell Ridge was Richard Stone, a valuable community leader. Before the town was built, there were several small chapels on the different ridges. One well remembered chapel is Laird's Chapel on Stinson Ridge. People walked miles up and down the ridges to attend church services when the weather permitted. (Courtesy of Margaret Matney.)

Clara Scott was a teacher and principal at the Jewell Ridge Elementary School in the mid-1940s. She later became a supervisor in the Tazewell County School System. The Jewell Ridge Parent-Teacher Association was an important partner with the school, and through the years, hundreds of parents helped supplement the curriculum with extra programs, adding to the recognized excellence of early education in Jewell Ridge. (Courtesy of Jewell Ridge Archives.)

Elizabeth Crenshaw came to Jewell Ridge to teach the third grade for the 1944–1945 school term. She was a former principal in the Montgomery County school system. (Courtesy of Jewell Ridge Archives.)

Gaye Harris taught at Jewell Ridge in the 1940s. She married an area native, Burton Smith, who was the son of Wallace Smith and brother of Roberta Smith. Roberta married one of the Jewell Ridge engineers and graduate of Virginia Polytechnic Institute, Gene Hilton. Going one step further, another engineer, Charles Hoover, married Gaye Harris' sister Kay, who also taught at Jewell Ridge. (Courtesy of Jewell Ridge Archives.)

Gem Kate Taylor began her teaching career in 1945 at Jewell Ridge. During the 1945–1946 school term, her co-teachers at the elementary school were Clara Scott, principal; Kathleen Harris; Helen Creasy; and Gaye Harris. (Courtesy of Jewell Ridge Archives.)

These ladies are seated in a classroom at the Jewell Ridge School. A 1940s Jewell Ridge Parent-Teachers Association meeting is about to be called to order. Among those pictured include, from left to right, the following: (first row) Lori Stallard and Elizabeth Shelton; (second row) unidentified; (third row) unidentified, Pat Howard, and ? Fox; (fourth row) Belle Burke, Tiny Kiser, and Mary Wise. The parents and company officials on the ridge were very involved in the education of their children and whole-heartedly supported the programs of the school and the Jewell Ridge Parent-Teacher Association. (Courtesy of Carol Mullins.)

Dorothy Scott taught kindergarten at Jewell Ridge, and it was truly a "child's garden" for these five-year-olds in 1932. Dressed for a program in front of their parents were (from left to right) Harry David Taylor, Kenneth Stanley, Harry Kenneth Smith, Earl "Skeezix" Fletcher, Junior Griffith, and Junior Joyce. (Courtesy of Harry David Taylor.)

Teachers in the June 1962 Bible school at the Presbyterian church were, from left to right, as follows: (first row) Laura Stallard, Cora McCracken, and Aileen Lockhart; (second row) Pansy Elswick Cole, Mary Elswick, Mildred Burke Patton, and Minnie Coker. (Courtesy of Bill Patton.)

Bert Edwards was one in a long line of ministers who served the Jewell Ridge Presbyterian Church. He and his daughter Brenda are standing on the steps in front of the church. This very active church was built after the 1936 town fire destroyed the older building. (Courtesy of Bill Patton.)

In the late 1920s, these residents posed together, probably after a church service or a school program because schoolteachers and preachers are included. They are (from left to right) Stan Smith, A. M. Christian, M. M. Burke, Belle Brewster Burke, Dorothy Scott, Edna VanDyke, Nancy Davis Smith, Robert Todd, Lapsley Liston, and Frank Zeigler. (Courtesy of John McClintock Jr.)

Five

LEISURE ON THE RIDGE

Dr. Huston St. Clair takes time out to bowl a line or two at the Jewell Ridge bowling alley. Along with his interests in the Jewell Ridge coal operations, Dr. St. Clair was a civic leader active throughout Virginia. He was named "Virginian of the Year" by the Virginia Chamber of Commerce. He and George W. St. Clair both served on the board of visitors at Washington and Lee University and were trustees of King College. Throughout their lives, they were active in the work of the Presbyterian Church. (Courtesy of Jewell Ridge Archives.)

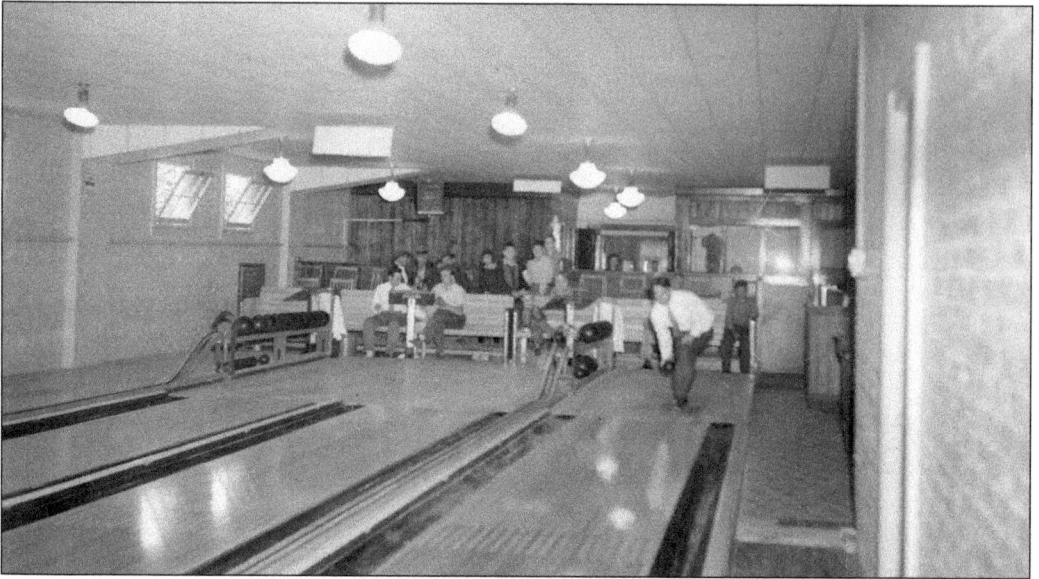

The well-appointed bowling facility sported four alleys. It was located next to the Green Fly restaurant, visible through the back window. On the ground floor, under the bowling alley, were meeting rooms that could only be used when the bowling alley was empty and quiet. (Courtesy of Jewell Ridge Archives.)

The Jewell Ridge Quartet entertains at the union hall in 1942 at a bond rally in support of the war effort. Members were (from left to right) Paul Cook, Omer Ketron, Ruth Burke, and Jimmy Herrell. The people looking on are unidentified. The tragedy at Pearl Harbor changed everyone, as it changed the nation. Young men left to serve their country. The Nester brothers, Marvin and Dale, were victims of the times. Dale lost his life in a training exercise, and Marvin was later a fugitive from the enemy in the Orient. Miners worked two and three straight shifts to meet the demands for fuel. (Courtesy of Carol Mullins.)

The Jewell Ridge Quartet (sometimes called the Clinch Valley Quartet) entertained for church, school, and community events for many years. Members were (from left to right) Harry David Taylor, Paul Cook, Allison Stallard, and Hobert Elswick. Singing, school plays, church pageants, and children's recitations were important in the early Jewell Ridge community. Before the coming of good roads and television, entertainment was largely provided by neighbors and family groups. (Courtesy of Carol Mullins.)

Students in the 1926 seventh grade at the Jewell Ridge School included, from left to right, the following: (first row) Claire Burke, Stella Patrick, and unidentified; (second row) Pete Patrick and Uva Kennedy; (third row) two unidentified. In 1931, Harley Patrick, a sixth grader, described his Jewell Ridge home in these words: "It is located on top of a beautiful mountain 3,500 feet above sea level. On one side of the town are Paint Lick Mountain and Clinch Mountain. On another side is Brown Ridge and toward the north is Chicken Ridge." (Courtesy of Carol Mullins.)

From left to right, Effie Brewster, ? Brown, and Lena Yost Burke stand under an important addition to early Jewell Ridge, the water tower. Behind them can be seen the tracks for the hoist used to bring supplies to the people living in the community. Burke was married to Thomas Burke, and they had three children, Hazel, Frances, and Mildred. The rarified mountain atmosphere helped create the clean, healthy town of Jewell Ridge high above the mining operation. It is said with pride that no coal dust ever settled in the homes on the ridge. (Courtesy of Bill Patton.)

During the years of World War II, a rally to promote savings bonds was held at the union hall. Grady Dalton, a Richlands businessman and a member of the Virginia House of Delegates, gave a rousing patriotic address. Dozens signed for payroll deductions to buy bonds, and youngsters were encouraged to buy savings stamps. The enthusiasm of the overflow crowd was contagious. Other participants in the program that day were the Reverend Nelson T. Barker, Aaron Russ, W. L. Painter, H. D. Hampton, Omer Ketron, Lee Burke, Howard Miller, John Sexton, and Rev. ? Wise. (Courtesy of Jewell Ridge Archives.)

At an elevation of 3,500 feet, Jewell Ridge gets heavy snowfalls. In fact, the surrounding areas often gauge the severity of the winter weather by what falls on the ridge. The snowdrifts are deep, and the roads are slick. Nevertheless, many early residents remember with much happiness the days of sleigh rides down the mountain. Stinson Ridge and Brown Ridge were ideal for long sleigh ride thrills. (Courtesy of Mary Elizabeth Jewell Henderson.)

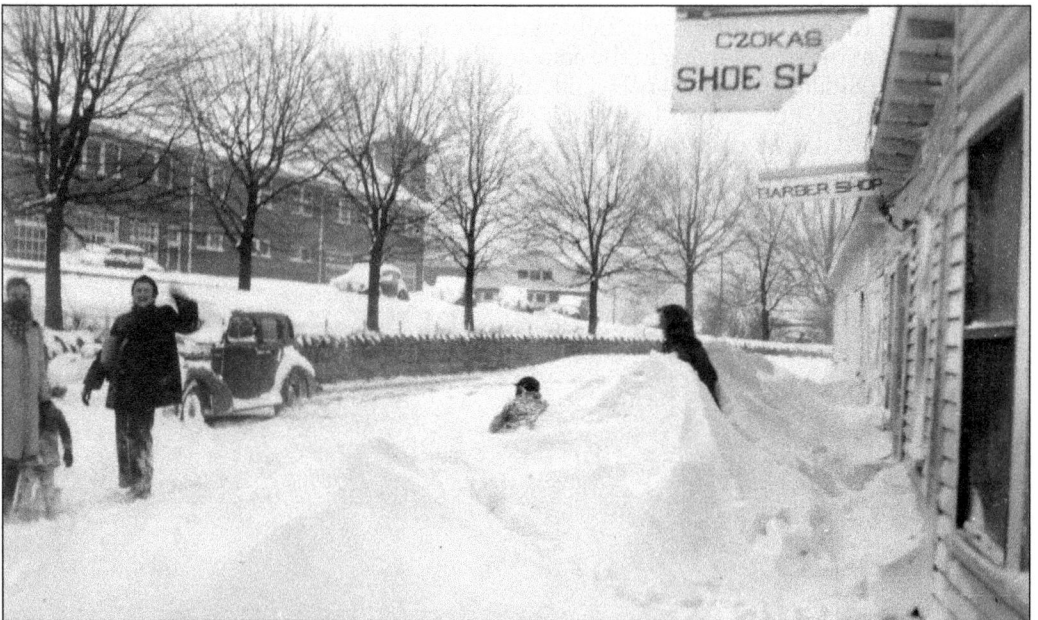

A day of snow, perhaps close to Christmas, was always a special time for Jewell Ridge children. The coal company treated each child in every household with a bag of nuts, fruit, and hard candy. Santa Claus used the store delivery truck to make his rounds. Many of the children grew up calling George W. St. Clair "Uncle George" because of his genuine interest and concern for those who lived in the town he established. This tradition was sustained by his son Dr. Huston St. Clair in later years. The "Christmas Treat," as it was called, continues today, with the members of the Jewell Ridge Volunteer Fire Department playing the role of Santa Claus. (Courtesy of Mary Elizabeth Jewell Henderson.)

Mack Smith (right) and Ron Penland stroll through town with a companion rarely seen outside the nearby farms. The yards and homes in Jewell Ridge were well kept. George W. St. Clair, who emphasized cleanliness and neatness in the camp, had trees planted in each yard. In addition, the family homes were known for their beautiful flowers and lawns. (Courtesy of Margaret Matney.)

Jean Joyce Saylors rode on the walkway with the assurance that all Jewell Ridge children felt in the early days of belonging to a community that was like an extended family. The majority of early miners were young men with new families. As a result, lasting bonds of friendship were formed. If there were disturbances in the town, the county deputy, Lester McMeans, took care of things. He was also known as the artist-in-residence. (Courtesy of Margaret Matney.)

Gladys Joyce and Bill Joyce rest in front of the clubhouse, a central meeting place in Jewell Ridge. The big building was a garage. Bill's car is a Chevrolet roadster. In the distance, the houses in Newtown can be seen. After the houses in Jewell Ridge were built, three other housing projects were completed: Newtown, Redtown, and Blacksburg. George W. St .Clair supervised the building of the homes and businesses, beginning in the early 1900s. (Courtesy of Margaret Matney.)

These well-dressed gentlemen are standing on the porch of the old store at Bearwallow. Only one man can be identified. On the far right is David Christian, son of Daniel Christian and the great-great grandfather of Scott Cole and Margaret Joyce Matney. (Courtesy of Margaret Matney.)

Gladys Davis Belcher (left) and "Sleepy" Belcher rest for a few minutes during one of the popular homecoming celebrations. Thousands come home for the festivities held every five years. The next homecoming was scheduled for 2009. (Courtesy of Margaret J. Matney.)

Pat Nearhood (left) and Geneva Nearhood Coleman are from one of the many Jewell Ridge families whose memories go back to the early days of the mines and the town. In April 1945, Cpl. Clint Nearhood Jr. was stationed with the army in Belgium. He was homesick for the ridge when he wrote the following to the newspaper: "The picture of Jewell Ridge with its one big street is fashioned in my mind. Every crook, turn and hump in it has a special place which I will always remember." (Courtesy of Margaret Matney.)

Friends relax on a summer day at Jewell Ridge when the weather is often perfect on the high mountain ridges. They are (from left to right) Loraine Johnson, Margaret J. Matney, and Helen Honaker Fletcher. (Courtesy of Margaret Matney.)

This emblem for the 1993 Jewell Ridge homecoming celebration, included in the sketches by Ellen Elmes, is a reminder of the thousands who come home to renew family and community ties each summer. The next homecoming was set for 2009. (Courtesy of Ellen Elmes.)

Loraine Joyce Johnson and Bill Robinette wait for a program to begin at a homecoming celebration. Before the homecomings were organized, Jewell Ridge had its annual Fourth of July celebration and parade. Thousands line the roads and fields to watch the spectacular fireworks display. The Jewell Ridge Volunteer Fire Department oversees the popular event. (Courtesy of Margaret Matney.)

When George W. St. Clair planned the unique town on the ridge, he must have had children in mind, as well as the welfare of the young parents. After a few years, a playground was laid out, and today the modern equipment still entices the young to enjoy play time in the park. (Courtesy of Margaret Matney.)

This quartet represents four family names in the Jewell Ridge area for several generations: (from left to right) Joe McGlothlin, Reba White McGlothlin, Bernard Gilbert, and Harry David Taylor. In the records of outstanding coal loaders for the first nine months at mine No. 1 in 1943 is the name of Link McGlothlin, with 3,361 tons. The other two highest records belonged to W. D. McHone and Lee Jessee. (Courtesy of Margaret Matney.)

The 1993 Jewell Ridge homecoming festivities were presided over by (from left to right) Robert H. Moore, grandson of George W. St. Clair; Barbara Altizer, leader of the homecoming program; and Thomas Righter, a descendant of Thomas M. Righter. Thousands of residents and visitors paid tribute to the founders of the corporation and to the families who have made Jewell Ridge their home. (Courtesy of Margaret Matney.)

These young people gathered in front of the union hall, or UMWA Building, to enjoy a warm summer afternoon. The only identified people in the photograph include Charles Blankenship (leaning against porch pole), Donald Shelton (standing in front of the porch window with white cap), and Drexel Anderson (holding hat in front of group). Jewell Ridge children grew up knowing they were safe and secure among family and friends in the extended family of their mountaintop community. (Courtesy of Jewell Ridge Archives.)

The Halloween carnival, sponsored by the Parent-Teacher Association and held in the decorated school gym, was enjoyed by everyone, including teachers (from left to right) Gaye Harris; her sister Kay Harris; Elizabeth Collins; and carnival attendees Eunice Lewis and her daughter Harriet. (Courtesy of Jewell Ridge Archives.)

C. M. "Bub" Brown was the recreation director for a long period at Jewell Ridge and endeared himself to hundreds of youngsters he coached and counseled in basketball, softball, and bowling. (Courtesy of Jewell Ridge Archives.)

The shuffle board courts were not used much in the winter, but they were popular places in the summer months. Just below the courts were horseshoe boxes where many people of all ages tried to make ringers, or "leaners." When snow covered the ridges, sleigh riding was enjoyed with great relish. (Courtesy of Jewell Ridge Archives.)

Narcie Hylton Smith (seated) celebrated her 90th birthday surrounded by her children. They are (from left to right) Bonnie, Princess, Katherine, Rufus, Roy, Edith, and Ann. Narcie Smith is remembered for her strength and determination. When Smith Ridge needed a water supply, she organized her neighbors into a force of diggers and plumbers, and got the job done. The governor personally congratulated her, and her reaction was "it's no big deal." Her family has continued her work for the community's welfare. (Courtesy of Katherine Richardson.)

Katherine Richardson was a contestant in the 1988 beauty pageant held during the homecoming celebration. The emcee at left is the Reverend Richard Stone. The woman standing in the back is Narcie Smith, mother of Katherine. Narcie brought the crowd to its feet when she swaggered on the stage to "walk the ramp." (Courtesy of Katherine Richardson.)

Marsha Stewart (on pony) and her father, Jesse Stewart, enjoy a day of sunshine on top of the mountain. Marsha is the granddaughter of Amie Lee and Jess Mullins, longtime residents of Jewell Ridge. Jesse Stewart worked for the coal company in 1935–1936. (Courtesy of Lynda Mayhorn.)

Roy Lee Smith is ready to drive away from his home on Smith Ridge. In the background is Brown Ridge. The ridges that make up the entire mountaintop community are named for the first families who settled them. (Courtesy of Katherine Richardson.)

Sunday afternoon on the front porch is a custom still relished in Jewell Ridge and other nearby communities. In 1959, the Mullins family enjoyed the day at their home on Chicken Ridge. The grandchildren are (seated) Jessceah (sic) Stewart, Mary Lee Ramey, and Lynda Stewart. In back, from left to right, are Jesse Stewart, Jess Mullins, Vol Mullins, and Hulda Mullins. Jess Mullins later bought three camp houses on Chicken Ridge. (Courtesy of Lynda Mayhorn.)

The grandchildren in the Mullins family got a treat during Sunday afternoon visits when they got to ride the ponies used in the mines. This was in 1954. From left to right are Jess Mullins, owner of the ponies; Jim Ramey; and Doug Ramey, a grandchild. (Courtesy of Lynda Mayhorn.)

The sports teams in Jewell Ridge excelled in competition and included nearly every boy in the community. The Jewell Ridge Red Raiders competed in the local football league. They are, from left to right, as follows: (first row) Jerry Lowe, Jay Hale, Eddie Russ, Larry Ratcliff, Eddie Griffith, and Chuck Kemp; (second row) Dewey Hale, ? VanDyke, unidentified, Allie Gibson, ? Gibson, and unidentified; (third row) Johnny Smith, Billy Goodwin, Douglas Roberts, G. Keene, unidentified, Sammy Farmer, Phillip Lowe, and Ken Russ. This was the 1953–1954 Jewell Ridge Red Raiders football squad. (Courtesy of John McClintock Jr.)

The Giants were the champion team in 1953 and won a trip to Richmond to play in a state competition. Team members include, from left to right, the following: (first row) unidentified, Jimmy Smith, Roy Hess, Darrel Ollis, Danny Jennelle, Jack Nipper, Teddy Hess, and James Kennedy; (second row) unidentified, Gene Gilbert, Wimpy Wise, unidentified, Doug Colston, Mac Blanton, and Johnny Barnett. (Courtesy of John McClintock Jr.)

In the mid-1950s, these Giants look ready to meet any competition that comes their way. They are, from left to right, the following: (first row) Mike McVey, Freddy Gilbert, Johnny Cordle, Ralph Griffith, James Griffith, Mike Bales, and Bobby VanDyke; (second row) Johnny Smith, Bryan Blanton, Jerry Lowe, Leroy Jennelle, Harold Buchanan, Walter Stapleton, Donny Shepherd, and Paul Gess. (Courtesy of John McClintock Jr.)

The Fourth of July fireworks can be seen for a great distance from Jewell Ridge. Thousands line the streets and watch from homes and buildings as the beautiful display lights up the sky. The Jewell Ridge Volunteer Fire Department presents the yearly spectacle. (Courtesy of Harry David Taylor.)

A sweet water spring, called the John Joyce Spring, was a popular visiting place at the bottom of tipple hill, an extremely steep location. It was also a place of mystery and of a robbery still remembered by old-timers in the community. In the mid-1940s, the spring was the site of a planned robbery of the mine payroll as it was delivered to the company office. Unknown to the robbers, one of their gang got cold feet and notified the authorities. The bank, in cooperation with the police, filled the money bags with shredded newspapers. When the robbers got to the John Joyce Spring, they were surprised by the empty money bags and the waiting police. There is also a mystery at the John Joyce Spring that does not have a resolution. On several occasions, it has been said, travelers have stopped at the spring to pick up a young lady who is hitchhiking. She is dressed in black and always sits in the back seat. When the driver reaches his destination, he turns to speak to the young lady, and the back seat is empty. Harry David Taylor made this artistic drawing of the spring as he remembered it as a boy. (Courtesy of Harry David Taylor.)

Visit us at
arcadiapublishing.com

www.ingramcontent.com/pod-product-compliance
Lightning Source LLC
Chambersburg PA
CBHW050639110426
42813CB00007B/1860